a PROMISE *of* SALT

a PROMISE *of* SALT

lorie MISECK

COTEAU BOOKS
WWW.COTEAUBOOKS.COM

Edited by Edna Alford.
Cover image: "Tree/Frost" by Takeshi Odawara/PHOTONICA.
Cover and book design by Duncan Campbell.
Printed and bound in Canada by Transcontinental Printing.

National Library of Canada Cataloguing in Publication Data

Miseck, Lorie, 1961-
A promise of salt

ISBN 1-55050-199-2

1. Miseck, Lorie, 1961- –Family. 2. Grief. I. Title.
PS8576.I815Z53 2002   C818'.5403   C2002-910315-0
PR9199.3.M4939Z47 2002

10 9 8 7 6 5 4 3 2 1

Coteau Books
401-2206 Dewdney Ave.
Regina, Saskatchewan
Canada   S4R 1H3

Available in the US from
General Distribution Services
4500 Witmer Industrial Estates
Niagara Falls, NY   14305-1386

The publisher gratefully acknowledges the financial assistance of the Saskatchewan Arts Board, the Canada Council for the Arts, including the Millennium Arts Fund, the Government of Canada through the Book Publishing Industry Development Program (BPIDP), and the City of Regina Arts Commission, for its publishing program.

For my family
blood and chosen

and for
Sheila Maureen Salter
February 17, 1953 – December 7, 1995

Where there is an unknowable there is a promise.
– THORNTON WILDER

But if the salt loses its saltiness,
how can it be made salty again?
– MATTHEW 5:13

IT'S DARK HERE. The room is small and there are no windows. Once I dreamt light, but it has flickered and fallen. And now my dreams bring me many things, but not light.

I think of the girl in the fairy tale, the matches, one by one struck against something hard. Was it flint? My fear is that she struck those matches against her own heart and that the moral was the heart becomes hard when it seeks light and doesn't find it. We used to have that story, remember, Hans Christian Andersen. We had many stories.

Remember the ones Dad told us about the King and his daughters, Sheila? There was always a king, always daughters and a bear or a wolf, some fanged beast the daughters would outwit. It was their cleverness that saved them. Not a man, or a weapon. The bear or wolf was never harmed, only shamed back into the forest and the daughters always made it back to the castle unscathed.

He doesn't tell these stories anymore. Not to me, not to our sisters, not to my daughters, not to his great grandchildren. Perhaps what happened breeds its own silence and each of us is sealed in a room like this. Quiet, how long has it been quiet?

How can what happened to you which was so public feel like such a dark secret? So horrible it can only be spoken of in quiet whispers.

I don't know what you remember of that day. Or if you remember at all. For me, memory has become mining. Has become core. Some days my memory is clear as freshly washed glass, and other days, blank as a new calendar. But I must tell you this, tell you what I remember. I must tell you this to remember.

THE STORY BEGINS in an old house in a northern Canadian city. For others this story might begin while in their car listening to the news. Or it might begin on a cold, dark morning in a darker parkade. Another version might start with a description of a woman's body found in an abandoned farmhouse. But this story begins in an old house, on an elm-lined street.

I want to say place doesn't matter, but each story needs a place. An opening scene, a beginning, a starting point. This city bursts at the seams with brilliant light and new green in the summer. But this isn't a summer story. It's winter, when the city falls towards the dark silent mouth of solstice.

It begins with a woman wallpapering her eldest daughter's room. It begins there and grows.

THE BALLET DANCERS on the wallpaper border remind me of Monet or Degas. They stand one by one, ringed in a delicacy of dabbed flowers. The dancers will live on the walls of my seven-year-old daughter's room. The border bought to complement the pale mauve paper for the top of the wall and a mint green for the bottom; both textured with marbling to hide the many flaws of the old plaster. The wallpaper, wrapped in my closet since last spring, has been shown to everyone who comes to my house. Later I see all the dancers, their long lithe bodies, their faces featureless. Their facelessness adds an ominous dimension, a haunting. A row of blank sadness. A silence.

I BEGIN MEASURING, begin remembering what a plumb line is. The level and square, the exacto knife, pencils, and a measuring tape litter the floor. I'm never quite sure how this works, and know I will make mistakes, cry in frustration and swear at myself for not watching Mom cover the walls of our rooms. She did it with such ease. Old white sheets drape the bed, the chair, and the dresser, which have been shoved to the centre of the room. The house is quiet except for the little clock radio with its crackling speaker.

OUTSIDE ICE FOG DIPS, covers the city, the street, and most of the province. The sky is as anaemic as the ground. Local news breaks the continuity of the morning. The investigation of the murder of a fourteen-year-old girl is finally closed. I remember her face, pretty and young, and the depth of her eyes, her picture on posters, solemn reminders pasted all along a jubilant street. How easy it is to slip in and out of other people's grief. An on-off switch, a channel changer, a newspaper crumpled in the bottom of the blue box. But I remember the search, the abandoned search, her mother's pleading voice adamant she was not a runaway, her mother continuing her own search. The brutal success of a mother's dedication. The sum of it, a dead and withered daughter in a grassy field months after she went missing. The accused killed himself before the police could arrest him, but much later, today, it is confirmed that his DNA was a match. Case closed.

Her mother's voice is strong and clear. I wonder what horror hides beneath her words. Inarticulate. Unspeakable. Are all horrors reduced to a thirty second sound bite, to three inches in the paper, next to the photograph of a beautiful young girl? I have wondered about the picture – was it taken at Christmas or maybe on her birthday, marking a celebration, then ending up on a light post on a busy street, in oily print in the newspaper next to the word *Missing.*

I STAND in my daughter's room, brush away these dangers, rape, murder. It never used to be this easy. Perhaps I'm tired, can no longer carry the weight of news stories. The weight it takes to fall apart. Perhaps I'm tired of fear and anger consuming me. I have retreated to my house where I can turn the dial of a television or radio, cancel the newspaper subscription. Instead, I wallpaper and paint. But something has made me listen. Something has made me hear. While I take in the words, I make a promise to my daughter. A promise that I'll make her room beautiful and bright, worthy of her, a place where her dreams will flourish, and where nightmares will be kept at bay. I put my heart's hope here, all my love and my prayers hidden in these walls.

I CAN SEE AN END to the paper and glue. I climb down the stepladder and try to look out the window. The view is obscured, etched with a pattern of frost across the glass. The temperature has not budged. Early in the day, I have taken a blow dryer to the pipes in the downstairs bathroom and have left the tap slightly running in the sink. A precaution. I don't want the pipes freezing again and bursting a valve in the washing machine like they did last winter. I sit in a corner of the room and drink my coffee, smoke a cigarette and ignore the uneven seams and the small bubbles appearing beneath the paper. She will be excited, will not see the flaws, only the brilliance of her new room.

I FINISH on December sixth. Wash down the new wallpaper, clean the hardwoods and pick up the remaining strips I have cut. On the radio, the mother of one of the victims in the Montreal massacre talks about her daughter, about the tragedy which has irrevocably reshaped her life. Her relief that her daughter was not shot in the face, the small mercy of that.

DECEMBER SEVENTH. This day has always carried a dark significance in our house. From my earliest memory of this day, I remember Dad sitting in the kitchen eating porridge, his hand cradling his head, his ear leaning into the radio. "Pearl Harbour Day," he'd say. And that was enough. Each year, he'd whisper, "Has it been that long?"

So this anniversary is stuck somewhere deep inside, not because of an interest in world history, but for what it revealed on Dad's face. Pearl Harbour, strange and beautiful words, unhinging something inside his chest. "That day changed my life," he'd mumble, then rise from the table and go to work.

DECEMBER SEVENTH. At first I think it's the alarm ringing and reach for the snooze button. The numbers 8:10. Somewhere beneath me on the main floor of the house, our youngest cries. Her screams escalate, climb to where my bedroom door is closed. She is yelling, "It's dark, it's dark, it's not morning, it's dark."

I drag myself from the bed, pull on a heavy terry towel robe and go downstairs. On the landing between the floors, I feel the cold draft of the old house. My daughter sits on her father's lap, stilled for a moment, but then her arms flail. She squirms and wrestles down from his lap. One by one he pulls the curtains back and reveals a thick coating of frost and the cool blue light of a winter morning. "See," he says, "it's morning." Her screams continue, without reprieve, through the making of my coffee, the packing of her older sister's lunch, the bundling of clothes, the kiss goodbye as her sister is picked up for school. I turn on the radio to listen for the weather forecast. Today, minus thirty degrees Celsius without factoring wind chill.

Nine o'clock and no distraction has worked. No videos, no Dr. Seuss, no *Good Night Moon,* no great green room. Nothing.

"Winter is like this," I tell her. "Always a little darker, but it's morning. Before you know it, summer will be here. Remember the mountains, we'll roast marshmallows, we'll go swimming."

Nothing works, dissipates despair, as she runs from room to room like Chicken Little. "It's dark, it's not morning."

WHEN HER TEARS STOP, I return to my room upstairs, to where the small thin blanket of heat has risen. I sit on my bed with my cup of coffee, fight the demons of a winter depression. My shoulders and arms ache. I am depleted by two days of wallpapering. Depleted by a child's screaming and my attempts at comfort which proved inadequate. Depleted by long cold days, endless dark days.

Each winter we ask ourselves why we live in this unforgiving climate. The sky is bland, the landscape white, with so little distinction between earth and air. Perhaps the sky has fallen. Perhaps this is what Chicken Little meant. Winter.

A FRIEND PHONES and invites me to a ceremony on Sunday. A small service before Christmas, to light candles for the dead. As I put the receiver down, the phone rings again. I assume my friend is calling me back. But it's Mom.

What is it about the voice? You know how you're told to look at the body gestures or the eyes of someone to determine if they're lying. You don't have to, you just have to listen to the voice. Even if the words are demanding deception, the voice will betray the lie. You have to listen. It might be a slight shift in breath, or a crack where tears fall out. Perhaps because the voice is housed above the heart and below the mind, it can't form an allegiance with one or the other. Its allegiance is to itself, within itself, within the body.

The voice is incapable of lying. Mom could have been saying, "I'm calling to say hi, how are the kids." Or she could have been saying, "I'm calling for a recipe." I couldn't hear her words, only her voice. Her words didn't matter, her voice was telling me everything.

SLOW MOTION. Remember the car accident I was in when time suspended itself? Pennies, which had dropped into the console over the years, lifted during impact and remained suspended in air, a frozen shower of copper. Mom says you have been abducted, Sheila. Then nothing.

I don't cry, but my body betrays me. It shakes, trembles, turns hot, then icy cold. It understands something my brain doesn't. My first thought is of you in high school, when you were a pageant princess. You were abducted and held "hostage" for a day at a fundraiser. I danced and cheered with another sister, that you were gone.

MOM HEARD IT ON THE RADIO. Not your name, but the address of your office and the description of your vehicle. She said she phoned your work and the voice of a shocked co-worker met hers. It's enough. We know. I hang up the phone. Walk to the mantel and light a tall white candle which flickers briefly, then goes out.

I HAVE LOST WORDS like trees lose leaves, winter loses heat and light. Where are my words? Are they here in this house which no longer looks like mine? Are they here? Anywhere? This is a word puzzle for the living. Empty and impossible.

I AM LISTENING FOR YOU. Shutting my eyes to see. Do you know what I see? The piggy bank you kept on your dresser years ago. The one the shape of three small monkeys, the first with his ears covered, the second with his eyes covered, the third with his mouth covered. *Hear no evil. See no evil. Speak no evil.*

Then darkness, and your voice saying, "Awe," the way you said it so many times, as a refrain to a story. *Awe.* Awe is all I hear.

THERE IS A MOMENT when I do nothing. Don't call anyone. If I stand perfectly still I can hold back time. As long as I do nothing, say nothing, hear nothing, nothing has happened. I stand in the middle of the living room, hold the cordless telephone in my cold hand. The furnace hums and the house creaks in response like old bones being warmed. I can hear my breath, hear my heart push blood through my body.

What is the body but a vast circuitry of nerves, a system of muscle, bone, and blood. An expansive interchange of cells, chemistry and energy all working in harmony. There is intricacy and intelligence inherent in our bodies, a stream of activity and cellular communication just to stand and walk across the room.

I try to make myself believe that you are travelling in a car with a man, cleverly negotiating your way out of fear and danger. Believe that it's robbery and you'll phone from a gas station somewhere outside of town. See your clever escape into the women's washroom writing *Help Me* in lipstick on the mirror. You're running. You're faster than him. You are outwitting the bear. More clever. See.

THE FAMILY HAS BEEN ARRIVING all afternoon.
Each time the front door opens and closes, heat leaves
and cold enters. The furnace cuts in and out. Boots of
various sizes and colours are piled in the corner near the
front entrance. Some stand next to their mate, others are
knocked down. Wool coats, parkas and ski jackets drape
the post of the bannister. Others pile up on our bed like
a sleeping body. I remember as a child, when we'd visit
someone's house, I would crawl under the coats on a bed
like this, and wake up the next morning in my own bed.
I want to crawl under these coats and wake up
somewhere else.

We don't say much. There is comfort in the common
sounds. The furnace, the hum of the fridge. Someone
has built a fire and wood pops and crackles. The coffee
pot gurgles and spits as it fills itself. I send my nephew
to the backyard where he splits birch logs into twos and
fours. The sound of the axe, the crack of the wood
splitting apart is as regular as the rhythm of a heartbeat.

Mom decides we'll be hungry soon and pulls a
chicken from the fridge. She has a way of feeding us
from food I would have discarded, or pushed to the back
corner of the fridge. She takes down Baba's soup pot and
fills it with water. I slice carrots, onions, and potatoes,
and peel the skin off garlic cloves.

Strangely it feels like a family holiday, a bizarre kind
of Christmas, Thanksgiving or Easter. I laugh at old,
tired family stories. I tell the story of how you chipped
my tooth. How you told me if I told Mom and Dad,

I'd get in trouble. How I held my mouth tight as a clamp for a day until hunger forced it open. Someone else tells about the pig eating your doll. For a moment, something near my heart lifts to these stories. Perhaps this is the purpose of memory. The purpose of stories.

THE PHONE RINGS AND RINGS as people hear about you on the news. As the calls come, I hear myself saying, "Thank you, it means so much. No I can think of nothing you can do." Some ask if they can join the search. Many say they'll pray.

Is there a prayer for this?

The house is sleepy like after a Christmas dinner. Some take naps, others pace the length of the living room. We bump into one another. Every now and then someone lets out a breath, a sigh, or inhales as a thought occurs to them. This is crazy. Maybe we forgot you had a meeting out of the office and right now you're sitting in a restaurant asking for a refill of tea. You are laughing, unaware we are gathered at my house, quiet as lit candles.

My husband's face turns ashen as he tells me he saw a white truck with a canopy down by the river. He knows it wasn't your truck, but somehow now he thinks maybe it was. This terrifies him. Did he drive by you? Was there something he could have done? We have all been doing this through the afternoon. It is the beginning of the *what if*.

At four our daughter arrives home from school, her cheeks rosy. She is surprised to see everyone at our house. "Hi Mom," falls from her mouth as she removes her winter boots and looks around as though she has missed a family party. I take her aside, try to find a place in the house where we can be alone. I take a deep breath and tell her something bad has happened to you. I tell her you went missing and the police are looking for you.

She looks at me and says, "Maybe she was kidnapped," and walks away. I have seen her do this before. She takes something in, keeps it to herself for awhile and then returns to me in tears or after a nightmare, sometimes days, sometimes weeks later. "Well actually," she adds, "she couldn't be kidnapped because she is not a kid." I hug her and she pulls away. I think of our aunt's death in a car accident. How for years car accidents were my biggest fear. Car accidents equalled death. "This is not normal," I tell her, "don't ever think this is normal. This is very rare." As though rare matters, when you are the statistic.

AN HOUR BEFORE the six o'clock news, a policeman calls to tell us they've found your vehicle. Have they found you, I ask, and he replies no. I know he can't say much, his cellphone is crackling in and out because of the cold weather. Nothing works in this weather. All he can offer me is, *Expect the worst.* His phone goes dead.

EACH TIME THE PHONE RINGS I hope you are on the line. This is what I do. Hope, and wait, and wait. In the absence of information, we turn the television on, and this becomes our source. Waiting for someone or something to tell what we know or don't know. The news anchor proudly claims they got "the story" first.

On this horrible, cold, full-mooned day, there are many tragedies. Robberies and beatings and murder. We are staring at the small brown box, hoping for answers. There are no answers. Just images, condensed, and small pulsings in the corner of the room.

THE NEWS IS A SERIES of quick images. The first shows your picture, the one taken in the summertime with your group from work. Trees, full and heavy with leaves, frame the photograph. A quick flash of light, then drops of blood on the parkade wall, on the concrete floor. Then your Chevy, tucked under a carport in another part of town. Yellow ribbons of police tape border the vehicle, smeared blood writes itself on the passenger door. An abstract of red, which I imagine came from a hand. Is it yours or his? Whose hand is this?

We watch the news in the living room. The photograph, the parkade, the Chevy, the handprint in blood. We watch, all of us together, sisters, husbands, children, Mom and Dad. Our silence is a hard bone. This is your blood, I think, but do not say aloud. This is my sister. This is my family. This is my house, my chair, my living room, I repeat these words again and again in my mind, as though I might forget everything.

WE SEND THE GIRLS to sleep at their cousins'. Friends have brought us salad, carrot soup and fresh buns from a bakery. We turn down the lights and burn candles. Outside the night is blue ink and we know men and women in heavy boots and snowsuits walk the moonlit woods of the river valley.

I want a ritual for this. My body moves to its own instinct. I follow. If there were a mirror in this house, I'd cover it with pale linen. If I found you and your eyes were open, I'd close them as one would draw delicate curtains, gently. I'd place coins on your eyes, and the egg-shaped stone I found on the coast, in your hand. Close your fist tight. Hold on.

I can't bear to sleep, my tightly strung mind is frightened by the dreams it may bring. Music strains from the stereo and the candlelight casts large shadows. We sit on our tattered couch, feet up, touching each other. The house is empty, yet I don't remember people leaving. Everyone else has returned home. We light more candles and I put one on the windowsill. We shut off all the lights in the house.

My right jaw is tender, feels bruised. We don't speak, except through occasional sobs, which the other responds to with a touch of a hand, or a sigh and an *I know*. Last fall we lost sight of tenderness, began pulling away from each other. Lost in our children, our roles, our responsibilities. This night I find him and he finds me. We find each other while you are missing.

OUR BED IS A FOREIGN PLACE and I can't settle. I slide from under the covers and move quietly to our oldest's room. I turn on the lamp and sit on the bed. You were here three nights before, in this room. I made you lie down on the new bed to feel its comfort. I unrolled the wallpaper to show you the colours, mauve, mint green.

I imagine pieces of you still here. Smell the pillow for your perfume. I look at the wallpaper, not the flaws, but the wash of colour. Ballerinas, faceless, stand as solemn witness. I talk to you, beg you to send any message to let us know where you are. The quiet answers me.

When I switch off the lights, the doors of the closet glow. I have forgotten that my daughter and I had put glow-in-the-dark stars and planets on her closet doors. I look at them glittering in the darkness. A blur of stars and bright beady planets. I look at the universe we have created.

THERE IS NO WORD for this cold. We have a pastime in this city where we try to convince each other and ourselves that the cold isn't as bad as other places. "At least it's not humid," we tell ourselves. "Yes it's cold, but it's a dry cold." This dry cold is a clever thief that robs our breath. To undress in the dark is to leave a trail of blue sparks. The dry cold in which hands and feet crack, faces flake and hair sticks to the head. But we say, "Of course minus ten with humidity would be worse."

Stasis. Stasis is the only word I can think of. Absolute zero, when everything is frozen, nothing moves. Cold perfected. The only evidence of life: pigeons huddled in a grey fist on top of my neighbour's chimney. The body of the landscape frozen, breathless. Consumed in a fury of white. How little I ask of these days riddled in ice fog. Blue unable to punctuate the long, grim sentence of a pewter sky. How little I ask of winter – just for the day to end – tomorrow to begin. Each day a new *X* on the calendar, next to yesterday's *X*. Waiting. *XXX.*

THERE IS A COMFORT in numbers. A rhythm, a pattern, a sequence. Always an expectation, a next, an answer. To go back is to pull against the tight-stitched sequence of time. Even there, numbers fill our old house. Five of us. Mom in the kitchen. Dad? Maybe in the living room watching Hockey Night in Canada. You have asked me to get something from your room. A book, or a sweater? I say no. You say you'll count, you'll time me, see how long it takes. My feet barely touch the stairs. Your voice is measured. One, two, three, four, five.

I LOOK AT A MAP of the city. Seven hundred square kilometres. Streets and avenues are the veins and arteries; the small white gaps are flesh. Silence. This city is a body unto itself and we are looking for you in it. A body within a body. Alleys, laneways, dumpsters are checked row by row, street by street. Checked in the North, South, East, West. No stone unturned.

Volunteer searchers have come from all over the province. One from the mountains where, a week before, they found a woman. She had wandered away from her group, but was found hours later dehydrated, chilled, alive.

They know they are looking for a body. A searcher tells a reporter, "We are doing this for the family."

Space. I've read it's the last North American luxury. I look at the map of this city, seven hundred square kilometres. You are somewhere in this luxury.

IN THE POLICE STATION I walk up to a man who has just come in from the bite of cold. He is tall, wears a red parka. The weather has turned his beard and moustache white. I say, "Thank you for volunteering. You are looking for my sister."

Each time I thumb back through the index of memory, I remember the look on his face, clearly. I regretted identifying myself. His look of horror, my words stitching his mouth closed. Speechless.

I can still feel his discomfort, can touch it and hold it in my palms. I reminded him he was looking for more than a body. He was looking for *some*body. He was looking for you.

I WANT TO REMEMBER the days that have fallen, to stand them up again, like many doors in a beautiful house. I want this house back. I want to go home.

WITH NUMBERS, there is no doubt, no possibility of confusion. To give something a name is to give it an end, but numbers go on forever. I'm four, lying on Mom and Dad's bed. I am counting. The sun is heavy and warm, the windows are open. Below, a radio plays in the kitchen, in the distance a train is switching cars on the track. There are birds singing, and the flies' wings hum. This is the only room I've known. I am in a holding pattern, waiting for one of the older ones to leave, to go to university, to get married, so I can move from this room into a room with a sister. I am counting, waiting for the numbers to end. They don't. They go on forever. I fall asleep.

I WANT TO REMEMBER EVERYTHING. I want to go back to the first train station I remember, although you are in the background. Dad took the job as station master in this town because this train station has running water. I always wondered where the Queen was when Dad told his stories about the King. She was probably doing laundry.

My first memory of you talking to me is when you walked into the room with a small black dog and said, "See our new dog." I was caged in Mom and Dad's room, in a crib with metal bars, my mouth pressed to the top bar. You had the most beautiful blue cat's-eye glasses. I know you hated them, but I always thought they were beautiful. I meowed at you when I wanted to make you mad. As you told me about the dog, he growled in play and tugged and chewed at the sleeve of your new sweater.

The next day, I went into the front yard after all of you had left for school. At first I thought it had snowed because it was so full of white. But it wasn't snow, it was the shredded remains of thread from what were once our lawn chairs and recliners. The metal frames were buried in the long curly strands of thread. I remember laughing and running into the house to show Mom what I'd found. It wasn't long before the dog disappeared. Many animals disappeared back then.

I'M NOT SURE what you know now. Not sure what you remember. If you still remember anything. Do you remember our black lab running up and down the gravel road with two ravens sitting on his back? How he ran the length of that road, back and forth, as the birds would fly and squawk, then land again on his back. This was their game.

I remember at night listening to the thin din of sound from your first portable record player. The Beatles, the Rolling Stones, Leonard Cohen, *Suzanne*. Your large poster of Pierre Trudeau above your bed, a rose in his lapel.

DOES EACH FAMILY CARRY STORIES unspoken in their veins? In ours, one would be the story of the robin. You were five or six, standing on the dewy grass with a salt shaker in your small fist. A few feet away from you stood a robin, and Dad in the background saying you could catch the bird with a few sprinkles of salt on its tail. You tried didn't you? Closer and closer. You tried didn't you? And that story became the story of betrayal, a broken promise, as the bird spread her wings and flew.

I FOUND A LETTER you wrote me after Betty's death. It slipped cleanly from a book I had lifted off the shelf. You told me you had trouble getting dressed. You said you were reading the dictionary, and were up to *L*s.

The truth is, Sheila, not one web draped in the darkest corner of my imagination told me I would lose another sister, suddenly. I thought there was a guarantee. We were immune. I have said half-heartedly to friends, I have an embarrassment of losses.

So here I am, writing to tell you I'm reading the dictionary. Did you know the word bereave means to be deprived of ruthlessly, robbed? That a reaver is one who robs.

I want to find the thief. I want you back.

SOMETIMES I WANT TO FORGET. Forgetting is reprieve, relief. I want memory to be stones I grind to dust. Hold my hands open and let it sift into the afternoon's crooked sunlight.

THEY ARE PROPOSING a mine outside a national park. I can't remember what they are mining for. Is it coal? I know this isn't central to the story. The story is what will be left. What happens when you tear down a mountain? When you blast stone away from the land? What happens to the trees, to the wildlife? What happens once you have found what you're looking for? What is left? A graveyard of rock and timber between you and what once was. They will move the discarded shards, spread them throughout the land, miles of creek and rivers choked with what can't be used.

OVERBURDEN. In geology this word is used to describe what covers the ore. Rock, clay, soil, trees. What is between here and there. Is that what is between us?

THERE'S A SALT MINE in Poland that dates back to the thirteenth century. The mouth of the mine opens to nine stories and three hundred kilometres of paths and caverns and pools. Beneath the earth there are chapels and statues of saints carved out of salt. Ceilings, floors, and walls of salt. At one time, bands held concerts there, and a huge chandelier made of salt glowed. I want to go there, sit deep in the earth, surround myself with salt.

CHRISTMAS. A tree is placed on our porch, food in boxes. Lasagne, casseroles, home-baked bread. Gifts are left for the girls. The day after your body was found I attended the school's Christmas concert. The children danced and sang; the only song I remember is *The Huron Carol*. I don't know why I went. Why didn't I cancel?

I sent the oldest to school through this. My need to pretend, to hold on to a thread of what was normal, was like holding tinsel in my hand. Shiny. Silver. Slippery.

We went to Costco to look for the last few items for the holidays. A father and a mother, harried and harassed. How I wished for that. When I turned my back he disappeared. I was nothing but a small dot in this great white concrete space. I couldn't find him. I looked around, looked for him near the bins of books, Barbies, the wrapping paper and bows. Everything glittered in this dead space. The air choked me, my throat was a dry stick. I turned and turned, but couldn't see him.

Remember when I was four and I crawled into the sweater bin in Woolworth's and fell asleep? How Mom looked for me? I wanted to crawl into something. A box, a dark shadowed space beneath the bookshelves.

I backed up and my spine pressed against the warmth of a man's back. I turned around and saw it was my husband's back. "Where have you been? Where did you go?" He said, "I didn't go anywhere, I was standing here all the time."

Everyone is disappearing before my eyes, except you.

I WANT A MAP of my life placed in front of me like a map at a mall. I want a map on a steel frame drawn in iridescent green on hard black plastic. Each memory sorted, placed in a location, a category. Four floors, one for the head, the heart, the body, the voice. A red dot telling me where I am so I won't get lost. Telling me I am here.

A TEPID GOLD LIGHT spills into the farmhouse. If this light were music it would be the mournful sound of a cello. I'm told by the policeman, "This is the spot. This is where your sister was found." I look down at the floor near the foot of an old wooden staircase, beneath a broken window.

There are many abandoned houses like this on the prairie. Echoes of time, of place, of history. They are the forgotten stories that lean and sag into the wind. Defeated by the sun. Ground into pale grey by the weather.

But even in abandonment, things are left. Not in haste, but with the clear understanding that they have outlived their usefulness. Redundant and repetitious items that have no place in the future. Wood stoves, stools, washboards, worn down over time. For others, these items are not redundant, but are the rare and raw treasures of the past. A salvaging. A reclamation.

THIS IS HOW YOU WERE FOUND. A Sunday afternoon, December 17, by a man who returned to his brother's old home to retrieve a stove. And what he came across was not the past, but the certain horror of the present. Your frozen and naked body, abandoned.

THE ROOM WAS STILL, except for a shimmering light and a slight breeze that lifted the threads of the sheer curtains, which have been left. These curtains once would have muted the sun into softer shades, but are now unravelling threads. The room was full of winter. A dusting of snow carpeted the floor.

I want to say I remember wallpaper. Yellow and white? Roses? Once, this was someone's home. This room, a living room.

I stood above the spot where you lay for ten days. Again, that feeling returned. I was chasing you and no matter how many days had passed, I felt as though I had missed you only by seconds, a breath away. I felt this way the first time I entered the parkade and stood near the blood on the grey surface of your parking stall. Felt it again when I helped clean out your clothes and found a Kleenex with your lipstick marks in the pocket of a blazer.

Beneath my feet, resting on a thin layer of snow, was a single red rose tied with ribbon. Someone had placed this flower here. I wondered who this person might be, wondered if I could find him or her to thank, to say...I don't know what.

SOMETIMES I WANT TO CUT the ache out of my heart, or fill it with something warm. I want to say this is not grief, say this ache is flu, nausea is hunger, and tears a lack of sleep. Say it is anything but what it really is. Say it again, say it often, find others who support the absence of grief. It's a virus going around. That's all it is.

If I make this an illness, I can look for a cure.

GO FOR A WALK, you'll feel better. Have you been for counselling? Try Reiki, try massage, try therapy, yoga. Art, music, movies, antidepressants, books, bereavement groups. Try anything, try it all, try it often. Get on with it. *Get over it.*

CHEKHOV WROTE, *If many remedies are prescribed for an illness, you may be certain that the illness has no cure.*

I WENT TO A CHILD'S BIRTHDAY PARTY on a quiet winter afternoon. While the children played in a room filled with red and yellow balloons, the parents sat around the dining-room table drinking coffee and picking the last few crumbs of cake off their plates. Shrill voices of children streaked through the air while a discussion about politics and books politely stayed at the table. One woman shared her passion for murder mysteries. Through a thin opening in my throat I said I was concerned about violence in books and films, without the treatment of violence at all. "Why would you worry about that?" she asked. She had heard about the murder, but hadn't tied it like a bright red balloon to a house, a home. I couldn't answer. That small thin opening in my throat closing. "You take things too seriously," she said.

WHY COULDN'T I ANSWER HER? Is it my body? Does its need to defer pain give birth to a silence so great it is rage? Inside me tantrums of thought pound my skull to the beat of my heart. I am at the mercy of my body and it refuses to give voice, to speak. It rebels against insensitivity disguised as logic, against those who have given up. It is the part of me which is not dead. Alive, very much alive. Kicking and screaming. While my voice remains silent.

WHAT HAPPENS WHEN NOTHING is mightier than the sword? What then words? Bent and twisted, frail against the reflection of the blade. What then?

HE HAD A DEVIL'S TATTOO on his shoulder, a tattoo of a woman's head on his arm, next to a sword.

THERE ARE MANY SHADES OF DARK, many degrees. There is a dark which is the colour of blindness, and it gags and binds and holds words under. But there are other kinds of dark.

The sweet gentle dark of shadow. This dark does not frighten me. What frightens me is fear and its seduction. Its cool persuasion convincing me to run blindly and silently to the safety of the nearest light. I am wary of the light I see now. Especially filtered light that fills my head with opinions and calls them truth: the newspaper, the television, the radio.

I am looking for the light behind the shadow. Shadows are always largest when they are nearest to the light.

PERHAPS I LISTENED TO too many answers, too many reasons, instead of asking questions. As a child I asked, only to have the question buried with reasons, rationales, or the thick wool of silence.

We grew up in a country of death and violence and cruelty. No war. This violence hid amongst the tamarack, the lodgepole pines, the aspens. It slept on the banks of the many rivers, the Peace, the Wapiti, the Smoky.

Sometimes it washed itself up on the shore in a plastic bag filled with kittens or puppies. Sometimes it screamed itself known on the last breath of a coyote that had been run to death by men in a pickup truck.

There are many stories I could tell of cats, dogs, other animals.

I remember as a child hearing about a bear who had been run to death by a skidoo. It must have been spring. I have drawn this scene in my mind and kept it there. Black bear, white snow, blue sky above. I can hear its breath, in and out, running to the rhythm of the skidoo. Running to the finish line, that last beat in its heart. I didn't know fear could do that. I wanted to know why the bear didn't stop, didn't give up. What I didn't ask is why someone would chase the bear to its death. For what purpose?

Now I read that a killer usually has a childhood littered with the carcasses of small animals. Littered with a history of torn wings, wrung necks, broken limbs.

I'VE BEEN TOLD OUR PRAIRIE WINTERS are exotic, that we who experience the hard fist of a prairie winter are unique. The rarity of this endurance proves a certain hardiness on our part. Maybe this is true, or maybe we are just fools, have forgotten we could live elsewhere. There is a book of poetry about winter. The first poem begins with *The generosity of snow, the way it forgives / transgression, filling in the many betrayals / and leaving the world exactly as it was.*

But I want nothing covered. I want none of the generosity of snow.

When you went missing I bartered with the sky, begged off clouds and weather systems, hexed the forecast, and prayed for what I hated: clear and cold. I did not want this transgression covered, betrayals filled in. I did not want forgiveness. Snow was the enemy, would cover tracks, blood, hair – anything, a small glimmer that would lead us to you. I did not want you left under the thick crust of winter. Discarded. A long dead carcass.

I REMEMBER WHEN I WAS A CHILD finding fishing line knotted. Amidst the transparent thread: hooks, several lures, grass and pieces of driftwood tangled together as though this was the likely outcome of these pieces, all elements of river life, man-made and natural, ending up together on the shore. Their entanglement was not the mystery to me, not even that they came together beneath the surface of the gaping brown river. The mystery was that they rose from beneath the depths and made it to shore.

I LOOK FOR YOU in this story, but you are always pages away. Ahead or behind me, sometimes near as the next word, or the next page. When I'm in the kitchen making soup with Mom, you are alive on another page in your bedroom with your small turntable turning. When I'm sitting in court staring down at my shoelaces, you are pages before, the heels of your shoes clicking against the floor of a parkade. And I know there are times your story is different than mine. This is an inverted story, beginning at the end. And if the story begins at the end, is it an untelling? An undoing? I've heard any story twice told is fiction.

PERHAPS IT'S NOT A STORY at all, but a bad made-for-
TV movie in its thousandth rerun on the only channel you
can receive. Characters so believable, they are not.
Unattractive bit parts add to the tension: bereaved sisters,
frightened children, shell-shocked husbands, parents split
at the core. The meltdown of a nuclear family.

TV REPORTERS USE YOUR FIRST NAME as if they have known you for years. We are silent, without a script of dialogue. They own you now. I sit in a restaurant, hear strangers at the next table speak your name, listen to them talk about you as if they know you too. I hear, "A friend of a friend was once in a course with her and she says..." or other variations on the theme. This is their privilege. This story has been sold, is selling. Night after night on the TV news, morning after morning in the newspapers. You are public domain. They know this woman who was murdered in a concrete parkade on a bitterly cold morning.

I quickly finish my coffee, put my coat on, and pay the bill. I want to find a place where I can be alone with you. But you are everywhere.

I ESCAPE EACH NIGHT into *Star Trek: The Next Generation*. Someone asks me how I've made it through the months following your death. *Star Trek* is all I can think about. Some look shocked when I tell them this. Such a small and ridiculous answer. But it is the future, the stars, where all of earth's problems have disappeared. There is hope and wisdom. There is intelligent life.

SNOW AND FRAGMENTS OF MOONLIGHT cast a blue haze in the room. We make love, sometimes twice a night in this waiting. This is what I don't tell people when they ask how I coped. There is desperation in our touch, our flesh, raw edges of passion. This is not an act of love; more an act of holding on, of the gentle mercy we find in each other's skin.

We both cry afterwards, but say nothing. Words seem useless, empty and cruel. We tenderly care for this time, hungrily protect our union, as though something spoken could take it away.

One time, words broke through my tears and I told him my sex had been damaged. Mine too, he said. There was nothing more to say.

WHEN THE DETAILS of your death started flooding in, my mind mopped them up into a series of images. If I shut my eyes while making love, the room disappeared. I was in the back of your Chevy Blazer and he was above me. There was blood everywhere. I couldn't speak.

I began to have body pain, beginning with my jaw and the sharp pain that ran up the back of my neck. When I sat in court and listened to the coroner detail the damage to your body from head to toe, I fell into your body, what was left. Each cut, scrape, stabbing echoed in me.

When he said your skull was fractured, front to back, your neck cut so deep your vocal cords, carotid artery, jugular vein severed and your spine chipped, a sound came from my throat. A tugging like an electrical cord being pulled out of the wall from a great distance. The same day, my own voice left and I was diagnosed with laryngitis. The doctor said, "Don't speak, say nothing for two weeks."

I ignored her and spoke in whispers. Each day my voice grew thinner until it was nothing but breath. My body in protest, silent protest.

ONE NIGHT THE TELEVISION SHOWED a protest in eastern Europe. A large group of women stood in front of a government building. They were silent, each holding a blank piece of paper in their hands. The women explained why they held the paper in their hands like small white flags. There were no words for their grief.

THE DAY AFTER YOU WENT MISSING I read the newspapers hoping I would learn a detail, a clue, something I didn't already know. Or maybe it was in that strange split of the mind, I could pretend that this was another woman, another family, another story and I could read each article, glean each word with a certain detachment.

When I opened one of the papers I saw your smiling face. Gripped in your hands, a gun. I had never seen this picture before. I had never seen you with a gun. The caption read, "This is a photo of missing city woman Sheila Salter that was released by police yesterday with no explanation of what she was doing in the photograph."

I sat holding the paper. I didn't understand this picture. I found out later it was taken in Phoenix at a western-style dinner for a convention. I have the photograph now. It's a full-length picture of you with a western belt around your waist and a matching holster attached to your hip. The one in the paper had been cropped and blown up to reveal only your laughing face, your hands holding a gun. You were playing a quick-draw game.

The newspaper removed the content, the context. In the series of photographs snapped in Phoenix, there is one of you, trying to rope a mechanical steer. Again you smiled, rope in hand. Why didn't the newspaper run that picture and say the photo was released "by police yesterday with no explanation of what she was doing in the photograph." There were many pictures of you, many choices. Why this one?

This was the first aftershock of betrayal. The photograph. Mom, upset, phoned the newspaper. They did not apologize for the distortion of the photograph. Instead they ran another story under the headline *Family Photo Bolsters Hunt*. Same photograph, cropped smaller, your smiling face, no gun. The first paragraph says that we hoped the photograph would help people recognize you. They explained it was a toy gun, what you were doing in the picture, that you hated guns and violence. They explained this the second time around.

My brother-in-law's neighbour, after seeing the photograph said, "I wonder what *really* happened, what that woman was *really* into." Mom in the grocery store, the clerk telling her with some empathy, "I see they got a picture of her in the parkade, at least she had a gun." My heart a magnet for these distractions.

THE NIGHT OF THE ARREST we sit on a ragged, stained futon waiting for midnight, for another episode of *Star Trek*. We turn on the TV early and see our faces, wet and strained, then a photograph of you holding your dog in a meadow mottled with spring flowers. We are the last of the national news. The news ends with the anchor saying, as he always does, "And that's the kind of day it was." That's the kind of day it was.

IT'S EASY TO HANG BLAME like a coat on a hook. Is it him, is it the system, the law, the media, me? But what if there are too many coats and too many hooks and you're too cold to take them off? Why is it I see transgressions at every turn? What of the other stories, ones written with wise and caring pens? They were there too. Written with compassion on the eve of the year's darkest day. A newspaper printed your poem about the robin, told stories of the searches and the searchers, of young people selling white ribbons in your honour, our gratitude.

YOU WERE IN THE WRONG PLACE at the wrong time. This is said again and again. I begin to say it. A friend corrects me. "She wasn't in the wrong place at the wrong time. He was. He was. Don't ever forget that."

WHY ARE WE ALWAYS looking for reasons for everything? What are we trying to prove? Nothing is random? Are we looking for a way to blame the victim so we can stay safe? So we can say to ourselves, well, I would never go there at that time. Oh, she shouldn't have been alone. What do you say about the woman who goes to work in the morning? She should have stayed home?

The woman at the funeral home is convinced you must have known the man arrested. I say no, and her face pales. I have made her vulnerable, unsafe. This could happen to her, her sister, her mother, daughter. Anyone.

THE TRUTH IS I could not understand how so much cruelty and kindness could live on the same street. People took our children, shopped for our Christmas gifts. Strangers and acquaintances alike would say, "Anything, anything. We'll do anything, just ask. Call us." They checked in on us, met at a community hall, and with kind and capable hands, buttered bread, made sandwiches and coffee for the search parties. It was as if you cracked open the hard shell of cruelty and in it there were warm beating hearts and many voices saying, "How can we help?"

Can only the body be taken and the rest, beyond possession? This is what he could not take: your essence, spread light and crystalline. It seemed as if it fell like salt on the frozen heart of the city.

WORDS ARE ALL THAT ARE LEFT. Small and empty. The inadequacy of this. I sit on my bed, cool January light is dormant, a sheet of ice. Such silence in winter. Bone-bare elms. Where do they place their memory of leaves? In the sap? Hard. A frozen lacquer. Is the memory of new green leaves unfurling in the trees' veins? The chickadee sings its winter song – a song of longing. Feeebeee, feeebeee, as though in grieving. Yet there is absence of terror or panic in their song. Longing is a given.

I THINK OF AUTOMATIC WRITING, the pen its own being, scratching on the surface of a blank page. I think of automatic living, stumbling and bumping through stores, our children's school. Smiling, a quick acknowledgement to women I see often but don't know their names. Meanwhile, our children share space, eight hours a day, nine months of the year, building friendships and histories. But the names remain unknown to me. I can't touch my life.

I try to act normal, but have lost the definition for normalcy. December 7, 1995, is a two-way mirror. A cut-off between now and then. When I look back, I see the other me wallpapering a daughter's room, tucking my girls into bed, randomly flicking through TV channels, complaining about the cold. I want to scream at that person, warn her, but I don't know what to say. There are no words for this.

A YEAR SINCE YOUR DEATH. I pace, pick up the phone to call you. It is only now I can think of the loss, feel it briefly. Loss is like touching cold metal outside in winter. First fingers sting, then burn, then nothing. In the past year, there was no place for this loss. There was no longing, just terror. No missing, just the panic of now. The now, the now, the now. Fear that I might forget to breathe, terror invoking a new demon – one who would lock all those I love in a closet. Shackle them in safety.

MAYBE I'VE LOCKED YOU IN A ROOM along with the dream I had after your body was found. You sat in a room with me, in a shade of blue so deep, I couldn't find the name for it. You were in your rocking chair, the wooden one, covered in green-and-white tapestry. I could hear your voice but your body was hooded in shadow. I said, "You're alive," then started to list all the people I had to tell.

You indulged me, encouraged me to make a list on foolscap. But then you asked me how I would explain your return. The more I explained, the more complicated it became, the more difficult. You didn't argue with me, instead encouraged me to write out the explanations. I finally gave up, threw the pen down in disgust, turned and left the room. I closed the door.

FRIENDS TELL ME not to watch certain TV programs or movies. *Cracker. Fargo. Pulp Fiction.* So much entertainment rests on the body. A body being found, a murder as plot, sometimes decorated with humour. A murder solved. A reason.

I'm frail in their eyes and need protection. When they tell me this, I want to ask – am I the only one who needs protection?

I DREAM OF CONTAMINATION. Above a gurney which I have been strapped to, two nurses in hard-pressed whites hover. They whisper to each other but say nothing to me. I'm not sure if I hear through their whispers or if I can read their minds. They say they must report me and warn anyone I have been in contact with. Full-blown contamination. Reptiles begin breaking through my skin. They are green, yellow, and red. I am infected, contaminated to the core.

I ASK MY HUSBAND if he believes filmmakers have a moral responsibility to their work. To what they show us, how they show us. "We all have moral responsibility," he answers. I had forgotten this. One month after my sister's frozen, naked body was found in an abandoned house, and I have forgotten this. I still have to ask.

THERE ARE PEOPLE I no longer talk with, no longer see. They have done nothing but spoken words. Words I deemed unforgivable. Perhaps conversations are like knitting sweaters. You do not notice mistakes when the sweater is done, complete in blue, green, or red stitches. But in the beginning, when you're casting on, you see each mistake as a gap, a space. This sweater is not complete. My body and eyes follow each row, anticipate where the error will occur. Days after the killer's arrest a friend tells me that what he did to you, must have been done to him. Not quite, I finish. He is alive. Knit one, purl two.

THERE ARE OTHERS I have not spoken to because their silence was unforgivable.

I SIT ON MY BED and write in a blue notebook. You are here amongst the lined pages, but I can't find you. My cigarette smoke is a blue snake twisting and turning upon itself. The long, continuous hum of the furnace is winter's chorus. It's night and the darkness which falls upon the window is a blackout curtain. Nights like this, times like this I would call you. You would lead me through this. The phone is silent.

IF MURDER IS WAR, and rape one of the spoils of war, I want this war named. I want it burned into the history books, studied and analyzed. Nightfall is our curfew, our siren. I want to run from my blacked-out home to a shelter, to hide from the silent bombs falling. If no one hears the tree fall, does it fall? If no one hears the bomb drop? I want this war named.

SOMETIMES WHEN I CALL MOM, she hears your voice. She tells me this – then a long, awkward pause. I try to find my voice, but cannot. You slowly climb out of my throat.

PERHAPS FRIENDSHIPS HAVE DIED with you. My heart is a beggar's tin can with a lid. But I will not accept any charity. One woman explained she didn't take a class because I might have been in it. "I couldn't handle it," she said. "It would have been too heavy."

I've deserted many friends and some, me. At a wedding months after your murder, I feel like Moses, can split the crowded room like the Red Sea. As I walk, from the corner of my eye, I can see people moving out of my line of vision. What power. What alienation.

BOOKS, NEWSLETTERS FROM SCHOOL, unpaid bills, coffee-stained mugs litter the kitchen counter. All this mess irrelevant. I take my right arm and start at one end of the counter, sweep everything onto the floor. The books hit the ceramic tile with a thud, and the coffee cups break. The loose sheets are the ones that float farthest from me, land last on the floor. I think I am screaming but no sound comes out. I cannot feel my arms or the glass which has wedged in my calloused heel. Just see drops of blood on the floor. No sound. A silent movie without music, in colour.

CONSIDER THE IMMIGRANT at the century's turn, leaving on a boat, hugging a mother, father, brother, sister...the final moment when the boat's anchor lifts, the last touch, eye contact. The knowing that this is a final goodbye. We now have technology to prevent this.

Technology has made death incomprehensible. I can pick up the phone and call a friend in Japan, e-mail Europe. These are our securities: they keep us from feeling the permanence of loss. Baba and Gido never had this. They knew as they stood on the ship in Danzig, their waves, their goodbyes, would be final. Goodbye has become light on our tongues. Always believing the ones we love are at the other end of a satellite connection, or of the ink on a page.

I HEAR THINGS DIFFERENTLY NOW, the strangest of details speak to the heart. On the radio a man tells about a plan to do a winter hunt of deer. Culling, they call it. The deer are starving, snow deeper than in past winters. Their gaunt tan bodies unmovable across the plains and foothills of southern Alberta. They have lost their energy to wander for food. Instead they take up residency under trees, their bodies curled to protect themselves from the cold.

A retired ecologist is asked for his opinion about the starving deer. This is the first time in years he has seen deer hungry and weak, and he and his wife have been feeding grain to the ones on their property. When asked if he agrees with a winter hunt, he responds slowly, asks us to look deeper, wonders aloud if there is something beneath the suggestion of the hunt, something nearer the surface than the dead grass which the deer cannot reach. He is concerned this is a lobby on the part of farmers because the deer that are strong enough are eating livestock grain. In a winter hunt, he says, we risk killing the healthy ones because they have the energy to make it to the roads and highways. Nature lets nothing go to waste he adds. The starving deer will be food for coyotes, shrews, magpies and even chickadees. Nothing is wasted in nature, he repeats, until man decides it has outlived its usefulness. The interviewer asks if we should let them starve? No, he replies, we should feed them.

ARE THESE THE WORDS I've lost: nature, hunger, feeding, responsibility? The ability to respond?

THE LAST SPRING you were here I watched two robins pick up dead grass and frail stems of last year's flowers in their beaks. They gathered the brown grass and made mud from soil and the puddle left from morning rain.

They built a nest on the back deck so close to the table that if I stood and stretched I could reach inside their perfect oval home. I phoned you that day.

Then four blue eggs, the colour of summer sky, sat safely beneath their feathers. One by one, small, almost bald heads with a few tufts of feathers appeared in the nest. You came and took pictures. Then later that summer, as though an afterthought occurred, robins nested in your hanging cedar box amongst lobelia and small daisies. They came to you without your coaxing, without a shaker, without the touch of a tail.

To look back at that summer my memory wants its own order of things. A system that makes sense, an explanation, a foreshadowing that knows its own light. There was a storm, one of those fierce summer storms that releases its rage as wind, lightning, thunder and hail. The robin gone from your flower box. Small eggs left like the saddest blue eyes.

Then the winter you went missing, there was a short TV news story about a robin that had not left its nest. Her red breast amongst all that white was like a drop of blood in the snow. She was barely moving, sitting low and patient in the naked winter branches of a tree. She refused to leave, instead nesting in cold silence.

I'VE READ, "Words cannot express what I feel..." in the cards and letters I have received. I've written the same myself. Are there no words for this? No language? If there isn't, why not? Why isn't that the question? This silence, this absence of language, keeps our houses divided. Language is our way of culling, the dark from the light.

PERHAPS IF I FIND A METAPHOR, I will find words, a way to explain. What is the metaphor for a woman whose voice was cut from her throat by a man with a kitchen knife?

BEFORE YOUR BODY WAS FOUND, the police had to determine whose blood was in the vehicle. They arrived at Mom and Dad's one cold Sunday. Two blood samples. Two red smears from those who are the source of you. My rage runs as red as their blood. All I think is, what else can be taken, what else? Now they take our parents' blood. When you were born at home there was so much blood, Dad stuffed the sheets down the outhouse hole. There has been so much blood.

While the police take the samples from Mom and Dad, a man is walking across a snow-covered field towards his brother's abandoned farmhouse. He is looking for an old wood stove.

IN COURT THEY CALLED YOU the *Blood Source*. In court there was a constitutional challenge for the subpoena of his blood. His lawyer argues that the subpoena violates the rights and dignity of his client's body. A pinprick to the finger.

There are other words I no longer understand. I leave the court and return home. Run up the stairs to my office. I pull out the dictionary, thumb the thin pages. I can hear the flick, flick, flick of my fingers as I tear at the pages. I want to understand. I've missed something, missed something.

The lawyer kept referring to the "transaction" between you and the killer. The transaction. Argued that it couldn't have been a sexual assault because you were probably dead. No sexual assault, at best tampering. Tampering. *Transaction.* n. transacting of business; piece of commercial or other dealing; in pl. reports of discussions and lectures at meetings of learned society.

MINUS THIRTY. I look into the backyard and see a grey ball in the snow. At first I think it's a toque, but then I notice it moves. A pigeon with puffed feathers sits in the only scrap of direct sunlight in our backyard. I wonder if she is the same bird that sits on the chimney above the second-storey room at the back of the house. The room was once a porch or a sunroom in summer, unusable in winter until a separate furnace was installed. The walls are almost entirely glass. In summer birds often fly into the windows. One time a meadowlark left a streak of blood across the glass.

But in winter chickadees dot the leafless branches of the trees, and pigeons roost on the chimney of the heater.

I bundle myself in my coat, winter boots, hat, and gloves, try to chase the bird, worried that one of the many cats which litter the neighbourhood will kill her. I try to chase her, slap my leather gloves together to see if she can fly. Her wings will not move, but she hobbles away from me, sits down near the back fence. I am helpless, home alone with girls and a car that hasn't started in days. Fly, I yell. Fly. She will not move, her red eyes stare back at me like two drops of blood. This animal is dying and I don't know what to do. The only thing my compassion for this injured bird has done is chase her out of the sunlight into dark shadows near the garbage can where she will freeze more quickly.

I don't know why I tell you this, even now as I pound the words onto the page. I question their relevance and importance. The long sentences of memory have been broken by lines, as though white space is the answer to a question I've yet to compose. Does any of this matter to you now?

FEBRUARY. I wake next to my daughter's skin, her feet tucking into my folds. This short month embraces the length of shadow.

I dress. Sometimes this is all the courage that is needed. Pants, a leg at a time. Grey socks, one with the sole threads thinning, the other with faulty elastic.

I wake to thoughts of Baba; the pieces of her left in me are like unpacked boxes in a crawl space. I wonder about her cousin who was shot in Poland. He was a writer, my father told me. I wonder about lives behind the names of family I've never met. Perhaps they are the key to another doorway.

What is it to be here anymore? In this frail bedroom. Windows of weak sun lighting the floor.

I LOOK FOR ANSWERS to atrocities in the old stories of blood, the wellspring of memory hidden from us by another language. Only the fine veins left. Baba waiting for her brother to return from the war of 1905.

No word from those men who fought the Japanese in Siberia. Thousands went but never returned. On horseback, trained to fight in the old ways, the charge of cavalry. They met a new world, and munitions. Bombs, guns that spit rounds of bullets. These peasant men far from home.

Her brother wanting to return to his family, thousands of miles away. The ache of distance and the scent of his wife's hair still in his hands. Each day men falling, each day the cries of hundreds of hearts echoing what the mind cannot articulate and the body cannot understand. All he can think of is the smoke rising from a chimney so far away, the hearth darkened by the shadow of history, the shadow of waiting.

The Tsar sent icons, to boost morale. What are icons against bombs, bullets, the falling of bodies? Against the memory of your wife's face?

TWO YEARS, DAD TELLS ME, two years it took Baba's brother to return. One day he just arrived in the orchard, resting arm against a crutch, his one leg blown away. He and his wife made wine and drank, made more wine and drank. That was the end of the story, Baba said.

Maybe I thought you'd return. We'd drink wine. That would be the end of the story.

THE DAY BEFORE YOU WENT MISSING feels like a month, the smells of wallpaper and solvent sting my nostrils, the radio voices of other tragedies, the crack and crunch of bitterly cold weather ring in my head. The day of the funeral feels like two months, and the five-week trial a year. Time is an illusion, does not really follow the linear track of our theories of minutes, hours, days, months. I have been lost in a calendar of months with no names.

WHAT IS COURAGE without context? Sometimes courage is opening eyes or sleeping late in the day, is entering a darkened parkade and its emptiness except for the sound of the jangle of keys, the shuffle of feet. Sometimes it's opening a small window in the heart and letting the black birds beat their furious wings. Sometimes it's letting in the daylight. The known routine of breakfast dishes, starting your car against winter's exaggerated darkness. Going to the bank, paying the phone bill, the power bill. Sometimes it's letting in the dark.

And sometimes it's simply saying this: I am lost here in my bed, amongst books and the trees' long bony shadows touching my skin, then retreating into the light. My house is empty of singing voices, but it is crowded with photographs, ornaments holding a skin of dust across the mantel, the cracked objects we bring with us from childhood forming a chorus of history, each insignificant without the other.

AND WHAT DO I WANT? If I tell what's happened, can we leave it there? Will that be enough to let me return to the rituals and duties of daily life? Return to laundry, cooking, our food.

I AM LOOKING FOR SOMETHING, a piece of a puzzle, a chip of something fallen away. I listen for your voice, which is held on the other side of time's glass. Read and reread the newspapers. Listen to the witnesses who heard you scream, *Leave me alone, just leave me alone.* I've listened until my ears bled lifeless, read until my eyes registered nothing further than space between lines.

Was it two who heard you scream? Two who hold your last words in dark memory. It's not their hearing that leaves a hole in my heart, it's what came next: silence.

I WANT THIS to be a ghost story. A ghost story, where the ghost speaks, jangles heavy chains, breaks windows from the inside out, opens and closes doors, writes messages on the walls, steals food from the pantry. I want this to be a ghost story, where the ghost will not sleep until something is put to rest.

I USED TO KNOW MYSELF. Who I was. What food I liked, what colour. I thought of myself as strong and fierce. A thinker on my feet. But when this happened, I could no longer navigate through the many banal decisions of the day. What to pack in a lunch. Orange juice or apple. Brown bread or white. To have a bath, to not have a bath. To get dressed or not get dressed. And if I decided to dress, I opened the drawers and became overwhelmed with choices. The blue sweater, the black T-shirt, the grey sweats? My body no longer fit my clothes. Nothing felt familiar, or comfortable. I didn't know which room to be in. Should I go downstairs or stay in bed? I looked for comfort, the way the body looks for the last position before it was jarred from sleep. Where was the hand? Were the legs outstretched or curled? I could not find my way back into that comfortable sleep.

BEFORE YOU WERE FOUND, I'd convinced myself your body was in the alley behind our house. I could not take the garbage out. I could not shovel the walks. I could not start the car. It was as if the air itself held a certain danger.

When we drove places, the houses and other buildings disappeared into a blur of wood, stucco and concrete. I counted alleys, the blue and green dumpsters, the vacant lots with overgrown dead grass peering dryly out of the snow. I had never been more aware of the many places one could hide a body.

THE FIRST WALK I took by myself was eight days after you went missing. I walked along a busy street. It was noon, and people were out doing errands. I was in the terrifying world of a small child. Don't talk to strangers, don't talk to strangers. But every time I passed a stranger, I wanted to say, "Did you kill my sister? Was it you?"

When someone pulled their hand out of their pocket holding keys, I saw a knife. When someone ran to catch the light, I thought they were running at me. The farther I got from my house the more my heart pounded, the more I felt as if I were drowning in air.

People say, *close to the edge. She is close to the edge.* And I knew I was, but I couldn't find my footing, I couldn't find where the edge ended and the descent began.

BEFORE HE WAS FOUND, I thought our house was being watched. That somehow he knew us, because the wound was so intentional, surely he must have been angry with you and with us. The deliberate rage. We must have done something wrong. Said the wrong thing. Been in the wrong place.

At night I could not be left alone in the house, even though the girls were company. We ran out of milk one night and I cried as my husband put on his boots to go to the store three blocks away. "Please don't leave me," I said. He called a neighbour who came and stayed with me for the ten minutes he was gone. I teased the neighbour about his babysitting rates, but my embarrassment was outweighed by my terror.

PERHAPS IF I GIVE THIS TO YOU, I will be done with it. Like a lover wracked with guilt from an affair who can no longer bear the heaviness of truth alone, whose only way out is to confess. That easy breath that fills the lungs, when the story is out, the confession out. But what is there to confess? That our last conversation was brief, my impatience pulling me off the phone, to the walls of my daughter's room. That I rushed you off the phone with a voice short and curt, that I never phoned you back as I said I would. That I never really said goodbye? What is there to confess? That there were nights I wished this on someone else? That this could have happened to someone else, but didn't? It could have happened to me, but didn't. It happened to you.

WHEN YOU FIRST went missing, we made trips to the police station. A news conference was held to make a plea to anyone who had seen anything. Hope knows no boundaries. We walked into the police station for the news conference – silence was a pain that fell in the room. Men and women, police officers, reporters, photographers stood in the fluorescent room.

I remembered a small town we lived in. After a car wreck, people filed by the crumpled car at the wrecker's yard. A strange procession, looking for blood, assessing the broken glass, the damage, and collectively sighing with relief that it was not them, not their family.

I leaned in and whispered, "We are the car wreck." Broken glass, crumpled metal, bent frame. We are all of that.

"THERE MUST BE a safer place than this. How can we live here anymore? It's safer in Dublin," my husband explains. "We used to be able to ride our bikes, and be out after dark. Maybe we should move." I tell him it's a time he remembers, an idea of safety, but not a place. I tell him that I too rode my bike and had a lot more freedom. He reminds me of the break-in we had. I remind him of the series of locks and alarm systems in his parents' house on a quiet Dublin street. He is convinced Ireland is safer. I am convinced no place is safe.

THE PHONE IS SUCH A STRANGE DEVICE. So much part of our daily existence. If the phone rings while I'm showering, I will jump out wet with shampoo in my hair and answer it, ignoring the stinging suds in my eyes. If I am outside shovelling, I will run across ice risking a fall, just to see who is at the other end.

One call can change everything. One call can change the course of a day, or the course of a life. There is an agreement with the phone, that we accept it into a life easily in the daylight hours. But if a ringing phone pulls us from sleep, either too late or too early in the day, fear replaces curiosity about who is calling.

Three weeks after your funeral, a call came in the dark part of morning. We were sleeping. My husband answered the phone, and I could hear a woman's voice at the other end, a slight lilt of an Irish accent.

I curled up in bed under the covers and the quiet. His voice was both low and sad. His sister was calling to let him know that their cousin, a woman in her forties, was abducted from her work. Later we learn her vehicle was found, then her body. Later we learn she was raped and stabbed in the heart.

I don't tell many people about his cousin. If this were fiction it would be too unbelievable. Even fiction demands limits to what the mind can take in, to what the mind can believe is plausible, conceivable.

WHEN I HAVEN'T SEEN acquaintances for awhile, they ask how I'm doing. It's not the words, but the tone which implies something greater. Your death was so public, our grief so public that I want to hide. I am embarrassed and embarrassed for my embarrassment. A strange notoriety.

I escaped the early days of shock and re-entered the world, where I was reminded and was a reminder. As though this is who I am. Sister of Murdered Woman. I have been introduced accidentally by your name, and one woman asked if I had been busy healing, as though this is my project, my responsibility, my duty. Some responses have left me separate, alone, able only to be with those who can touch the scariest part of themselves and others, and still stand.

THIS IS THE PROBLEM. I have been angered by those who have treated your death, and my grief, as something that should never be talked about. A private affliction that I am supposed to carry, but not mention. Yet, others may have been wise to keep their words to themselves, as one line misspoken has left my heart without charity or forgiveness.

But I am the problem. I am the one who tells me to be quiet, speechless, silent. I am the one.

I MISS COMING HOME on a Saturday afternoon from errands and seeing your car out in front of the house. You inside, laughing, telling the kids a story, or some small incident or dream which would have seemed insignificant to most, but one where you discovered profound meaning. Your dream of the wasp, hovering effortlessly, in sunlight. How it released your pain around Betty's death. It gave back your freedom. Now I'm left with the dilemma of whether to kill or capture the ones that enter my house. I miss your clarity. I miss your utter trust in the world and all its goodness.

I miss going with you to the New Age bookshop near the house and looking at many divination systems. Tarot, animal, spiritual path cards. I miss swapping books, the ones that say trust the universe on every second page. I want to believe that one person can cause as much good as pain. I want to believe you still, when you told me there are no accidents.

I went back to that bookstore, months after your murder, looking for bereavement books. This time the soft gel of music and the smell of aromatherapy oils left me with a headache. There were only a few books on grief, as though bereavement is somehow not related to the spirit or the spiritual world. I asked a woman to help me find books about violent crime and bereavement. I told her what happened to you. She asked me if I believed in karma, and I knew what was coming next. I held my breath. "Your sister murdered someone in a past life," she said.

I WANT THIS TO BE a murder mystery. Where notes are taken over dinner, over glasses of wine, the best Alberta beef. Succulent and rare. Over Caesar salad, tomatoes and cilantro. A game with clues. Remember? Colonel Mustard in the dining room with a knife. Miss Scarlet in the ballroom with a lead pipe. Professor Peacock, a gun. A game, a roll of dice. No motive, no victim. Just the process of elimination. The game ends. The board is closed like a door. The pieces put back in a bag, then boxed and put away in the closet. There is a winner.

LET ME EXPLAIN HOW UGLINESS becomes a particular beauty when you look away, the reprieve of an eye unstrained.

They say when you look at something long enough it transforms, you begin to see the colour shaping, the background and foreground haloed in your sight. All becomes part of your vision, worthy of no more or no less attention, another detail in the landscape.

Look at the woman who believes wallpaper could change her daughter's room, soften the view to the very hard world. Marbled paper to conceal these old walls that bulge the way a body does when it's almost finished. Look at the woman whose own romance has become thin as her gold ring, yet covers cracks with a cotton candy sensibility, mauve and mint green, wrapping the room with a border of ballet dancers, their quiet pliés, as if Monet or Degas, born today, would be interior decorators. Listen to the crackle of the radio, cutting the soft edges of light. There are wars out there, and murders happening on some unknown street, and more wars, and beatings all culled into thirty-second sound bites entering this space.

THIS IS WHAT I DO while I sit in the courtroom. This is what I do when I stop counting the words of lawyers and witnesses and the judge. Words that fly black and big and brilliantly above my head. Singing in my ears, ringing in my ears – their cries similar, each with their own weight, yet all weighing the same. A group of crows flying. A group of crows crying. What is a group of crows? A murder.

This is what I do, how I navigate this place. This place of reverence for the word. Reverence for the law and the argument. I run my eyes up and down the spine of his lawyer, imagining each glance is one pain. Then two, then three. The accused is from another world and I have no atlas. And he does not speak. But this one, this lawyer, I understand. We have read the legends of the same maps. His job, a cool and concise negotiation of words, of events, of acts. And everyone is entitled to a defence.

Is this what I've done? Negotiated words, measured them, weighed, put them in the right order? Before this happened, is this how I slept at night?

I hear him say, "Certainly, murder is never pleasant." Each word bled dry and passionless.

WHEN I EXPRESS MY FURY about this man in the grey suit, I'm told by a friend he's just doing his job. What is this job, where all acts become civil, negotiated, and sanitized? "You have to understand the process, you have to understand. It's imperfect, but it's the best system we have." I don't want to talk of systems, their imperfections. I don't want to talk. I don't want to understand.

THIS IS WHAT I DO in the stale, sickly air of the courtroom. I look at his lawyer's back and imagine him as a boy, his face stuck in books. Oh he loved those words, the beauty of each sound opening his mouth to the world of possibility. He learned the words: integrity and honour and argument. His mother pressing his Sunday suit while he read *To Kill A Mockingbird* for the fourth time. His dog, Scout, and his cat, Atticus, both at his feet, sharing the one small piece of light from a narrow window.

THERE ARE NO WINDOWS in this courtroom. No
sunlight.

AFTER THE TRIAL ENDS there is talk of closure. Guilty. Is it over? I sleep late. A friend phones and tells me about a morning radio contest. They have taken a voice from our family and played it with the clue, "salt in the wound." This clever play on your name. This clever sting. If a listener can identify the voice, tie the news item to the person speaking, they will win. What? A ball cap? A coffee mug? A bumper sticker? There is a winner.

I spoke with the producer, who had been away when the contest ran. He apologized. But it wasn't the apology that brought relief, it was the humanity.

THIS IS WHAT I DON'T want to remember. Your body. What the snow and cold took and what it left. I don't want to remember makeup, all the mortician's makeup that couldn't conceal what it covered. I circled the casket again and again, trying different angles, trying to capture you. It's as if you've been taken too many times, that nothing is left but a brittle shell. My eyes are perfect apertures, but the film in my mind is overexposed, erased. I wanted to touch you, your hand, your arm, but couldn't, felt if I did, something would break. As if I were in an expensive jewellery shop with a sign that says, *anything you break you have to pay for.*

ROUND AND ROUND AND ROUND I circled while Dad swayed. When I gave up looking for something that might make me recognize you, I saw Dad. How small he is. Age and time and the sharp edges of experience have taken his height. His face is ravaged with something near despair, but different and darker. Where are his stories now?

The room blurred to stillness. He moved towards me in a helpless faltering, holding out his rough hands, and said, *Who could do this?* I stepped back from him. I stepped back, not forward, knowing that if I touched him we both would fall. Everything is breakable. Everyone.

I WANT TO REMEMBER everything, but words have fallen into the dark eye. The dark I. I want to remember your face, before. Not what was left. How swollen it was under the makeup. And the scarves, the two scarves that wrapped your neck, their feeble attempt at kindness to hide what was underneath. That terrible opening, a black mouth.

Your hands always so beautiful, painted and articulate; now small, mute and white as dough from a bitter bread. Nails chipped and cut, and dried scratches on the knuckles, on the wrists. Your hands spoke one last time, grasping a new and cruel language.

MY FRIEND SAYS, "How could you see her like that. How could you?" How could I not. How could we leave you captured in his eyes, his memory. How could we leave you with a stranger. You had to come home. To us.

THERE WAS NOT ONLY TERROR, but tenderness. We were given pictures as we left the funeral home. Taken a month before, the week before you went missing. I carried the envelope of pictures in my purse. I framed the one of you standing on the red rock of desert. You are wearing sandals, T-shirt and shorts and sunglasses. The sky is so blue, rock so red it burns. I want to say resplendent. You are looking out, past the edge of the picture. You are smiling as you watch something on your right.

AFTER THE FUNERAL, I stayed in bed for days and days, and months. I have read that death awakens the dead in you. And you had. I slept. And slept. I slept while my ghost crawled out of my bones each day and dressed before the children came home. The ghost washed her hair, her body, her feet so tenderly it left no mark. The ghost drew a smile on her face with lipstick and made meals, read them stories and pretended she was their mother, while I slept.

The girls knew something was different about their mother. More subdued, a quieter version of the one they remembered. But they let her sleep, believing in an antidote for the spell of the poison apple. The ghost baked layer cakes each week. French chocolate, lemon, orange, spice. Each week another cake, another layer.

MY OLDEST DAUGHTER watched me sleep. And sometimes she would keep me awake with stories from her dreams. Once she crawled into my bed crying. She said she had a dream about you, and I told her I knew how scary dreams could be.

"No," she said, "no, the dream was not scary. She brought me a horse and told me the treasure was in the North."

"If it wasn't·scary," I asked, "then why are you crying?"

"Because when I woke up, I remembered she was dead."

IN SCHOOL OUR DAUGHTER IS TAUGHT how to decipher facts, how to critically analyze clues. In science she learns this as part of *Evidence and Investigation.* Field trips are planned to enhance the course. One possibility is the science centre. They have a display, a murder scene. Many of the field trips offered for this unit are murder scenes. Murder is more than a game, it's a learning tool.

I want to see this display before she goes with the school. I pay my seven dollars and walk up the stairs to the display. It is a set decorated to resemble a rundown rooming house. In the entrance is a mannequin dressed up like a police officer. Above the door, and below a stop sign, is a warning that this might be upsetting to some.

I enter. The first room is a rundown kitchen where two mannequins sit at the table. Press a button and they talk. The policeman is taking evidence; the other is a witness. The next room, the bedroom, is the murder scene. Again, mannequins dressed in white forensic uniforms are gathering evidence. Press a button and a recorded voice rings in the room. "I'll never get used to the smell." The body has been removed, just a chalk line left. The mattress, stripped of sheets, is soaked in blood. The faded wallpaper is sprayed with blood. A small Polaroid of a man lying face down with a bullet hole in his back is left in the room, next to a form forensic units would use to detail the body. Humidity is mentioned, as are bugs in the body. Also a clue.

My knees buckle in response to two men who now stand behind me. "Cool," the one says to the other. "Look at all the blood, cool."

I CALLED THE SCIENCE CENTRE and asked if they considered the age of the children who will see this display. The man tells me of course they did. He asks me if I noticed there is no reference to drugs or alcohol. I tell the man that I am not concerned about drugs and alcohol. I tell him I'm concerned about the imagery, the effect that it may have on ten-year-olds. He responded, "It's not real blood, it's paint."

I tell him that many children this age are not allowed to see movies because of the violent imagery. I tell him that many children are frightened by violence; with the latest rash of killings in schools, gang killings in this city, they are frightened.

He tells me this display does not depict violence, it depicts the aftermath of violence. The conversation played itself out, and I played myself out. Speechless, again.

The principal and the science teacher find another field trip. One without blood, or a body. I feel something warm in my throat. A sound rising into my mouth, my words spoken in my own voice. *Thank you.*

BUT FOR THE MOST PART, each day I lost more language, lost more words as if they flew from the house. Left with each breath. Left through a door ajar. Through the vents, the small cracks in the old house. Flew through the phone line, through the wires, and formed as black birds in the bare branches of elms. They left daily, as new betrayals entered the house disguised as words.

I'd climb the stairs and find the black garbage bag I secretly stored in the closet. Spill the contents on the floor. Stale and yellowed newspapers and a box brimming with cards and condolences. I'd read, re-read words cast by strangers, cast in dark ink on newsprint.

There is an article that says crimes like this aren't supposed to happen to a family like yours. Then who? Who should they happen to?

Photographs harsh and human colour the pages. The farmhouse, the funeral, our family. A picture of Mom and Dad so heartbreakingly beautiful in its truth, their grief.

This is where I keep what's left of you. Unable to let go. This bag is my source and my sorrow.

THERE ARE WORDS that break you and words so simple they mend. The girls stood at the foot of my bed, said, "Mom, please come back."

I WANT TO TELL YOU his name and then I can be done. You are the only one who doesn't know his name. To name something is to give it containment. I want to tell you how his name came apart in my chest on a cold night, a constellation of red stars.

BRIGHTEYES.

IN MY SLEEP I FLOATED. Floated in tears. My body spread across the water in the shape of a star. Somewhere in the distance on the edge of the shore was my family. I could hear them make plans, hear the doors of the house opening and closing. Their voices spilling across the water like dark ink.

I remembered a time before, when there were no words, just the gentle lapping of the salt water of the sea. And what was left as a reminder of the journey from sea to shore, from the climb out of the mud to crawling, then standing, then walking, was the salt water left in the tears and water of the body. How my daughters had floated inside me in the same salt water. I remembered salt, the taste on the tongue, the medicine it gave to heal the body when mixed with water. The sting of salt in the wound. Where was the antiseptic now, the cleansing, the purification?

Perhaps Lot's wife knew this instinctively. Perhaps turning to salt was the only solution.

WE WENT TO IRELAND and visited with friends who have moved into the country to a quieter, simpler life. The woman tells me about her sister, how much she loves her and thinks her desire to see her more is not mutual. Her sister is older and doesn't have the same need. I tell her about being the youngest of five girls, how I ached to have them notice me, ached to have that desire returned.

As we walked up a soft path, avoiding the gorse thorns which pricked our legs, we talked about our lives. She hasn't seen me since your murder. She stops near the top of a hill and asks how I'm really doing.

I tell her the past year was hard. That I'm either angry, or so depressed I am fatigued. I tell her I have stopped believing grief has a shelf life. That I've tried to put this somewhere but it won't go away. And I realize no matter how much time passes, there are some days the wound is so fresh it paralyzes me. That the pain will never go away, no matter what I do.

"So you're telling me you've accepted her death," she says.

I stop, a bit breathless from the climb and say, "I guess I am." I guess I have.

ON THIS TRIP TO IRELAND I want to find the grave of the cousin. We stop at a shop in a small town near where the murder occurred. The shopkeeper we ask knows which cemetery. There is an expression on her face, a knowing that says this murder is still an open wound. I buy a bouquet of flowers, pink, white, yellow. We take directions and drive down narrow back roads.

We walk the rows looking for the name and I find the grave. The top has been cleared into a small garden and someone has planted flowers. On the headstone, her name, date of birth, date of death, and words that I've been looking for. Words to sum up what has happened to her. Words boldly etched on grey stone. *Cruelly Taken.* Bereaved.

IN THIS NORTHERN CITY summer returns slowly. I sit on the front porch and open the newspaper. The truth is I have lost count. Is it three, four, or maybe five years? I have to think about it, calculate. Subtract.

There is stillness in the early Sunday morning. I take a breath, breathe in the greening. I have begun to read the paper again in that old way. The way that says this isn't about me.

I thumb through the entertainment section, pass pictures of strangers. Near the centre of the paper, there is a black and white photograph of a woman's sweater. It may have been cream, white, or tan. The sweater is on a hanger, the sleeves extended. I turn the page, but something makes me hesistate. Or perhaps it's my heart, that small nervous flutter, the familiar wings of terror beginning to beat. I turn back to the page.

Most of the sweater is stained, darkened. The caption says it's blood. A chill slowly climbs up my spine as my eyes scan down the line of text to a photograph of you. And him. This is the way it has been. Your face, next to his. Inseparable. Captured. In the upper left corner, a tag is pinned near your sweater with a number: 95-107828. This is your sweater, your number. I want to say I remember that sweater. Remember, you wore it the night we went to the Greek restaurant. I had souvlaki, you had the fried cheese. But I don't. I don't know the colour. I don't remember the knitted pattern.

Your face surrounded by two pages about forensic science. This story says they use your case as a teaching tool for police. Your sweater, photographs. Patterns of blood will tell what has happened at a crime scene. The police here are being trained to listen.

Every now and then, this story of a woman murdered returns, resurfaces, gasping for air, then disappears into yesterday's news.

I WALK WHEN THE NIGHT is light with summer as though a heavy lid has been lifted off the sky. The new green leaves, the new limbs of trees wet and supple with sap, and the fresh scent of the first flowers deny any past. Deny any history, as though there has only been this moment.

As I walk, I talk out loud. Sometimes to you, sometimes to the air, as if I am rehearsing a speech, learning the lines.

Mom used to talk out loud. She would stand in the basement, pull wet clothes through the wringer washer and talk. Silent, I would watch from my step on the basement stairs. Her arms gesticulating, her words breathy, yet with authority. I always wondered who she spoke to. What was the name of her imaginary friend and sometimes foe.

Now I realize it was grief she spoke to. That familiar ache, so silent but listening, waiting for the words.

I NO LONGER LOOK for simple explanations, though there are moments I crave them. I don't want to say, "Why you?" or "Why us?" There would be too many people walking on this planet asking the same question. You always said there were no accidents. What do I call this, then?

I want to put it all in a box, in a room, and lock the door. But it is too messy, too uncontainable. It bleeds and stains everything. Your death and the way it happened inform my life. It is the paint and paper of my house. The floors, the walls, the ceilings. It is the street, the avenues, and the intersections I travel.

I can't separate you from what happened, or what happened from you. I've tried. I put your dying on hold, thinking when the trial ended, when that was done, the murder would disappear.

I convinced myself I could accept your dying, but not the way you died. As though I could separate the two like yolk from white. On other days I could accept the vicious act, but not that it happened to you. This only happens to someone else, someone you don't know. Someone you read about in the newspaper, someone you see on the television news or talk about in a restaurant with interest and speculation, providing your own scenarios of what really happened.

But I know now that to deny one part and not the other is a half-truth, thus a half-lie. To deny either is to deny your history and now mine.

THERE IS NO RESOLUTION. Only resolve. Words holding themselves against the page as though it were a mirror. Saying we are not leaving. Look at us. Look at us, have we said what can't be said? Are we beautiful? Resolve, the last chord of a song that takes dissonance to consonance.

IN THE LOW BOUGH of a spruce tree a robin built her nest. Dad says it's unusual for robins to nest so near the ground. I have not seen a nest this clearly and closely since the one in the backyard years before. I watch her from the front porch. Sometimes when I come home from work the nest is empty and my heart quickens, but then I hear her and her mate's low notes and she returns. They have taken turns warming the eggs. This time there are not four eggs, only two.

I am trying not to make this an omen, but there was relief in my heart when I saw the two chicks' heads peek out. I am trying to make this what it is. Nature revealing the delicacies of spring. Sometimes when the mother leaves the chicks, I have to wait and watch. I keep an eye on the neighbour's cat, the noisy jays and two magpies that are completely at home in our yard. I watch. I listen. I wait for the familiar sound of her wings, her soft song as she returns to the nest. This is all I can do. Watch and hope a little.

AUTUMN. On my neighbour's roof a cat perches on the last branch of sunlight. Higher than any birds today, which swoop and swoon close to the ground, retrieving the last cache of seeds and berries. Beneath, brown leaves rustle with the requests of mice. They want a home.

October smells of decay. Each day is less a promise than a certainty. The cat watches from the roof with indifference. She is full this hour, satiated.

Things I've wanted to say have vanished without being said. Clouds move in from the north and take with them the light and the last few crumbs of heat. Our oldest daughter turned twelve last week and she is now as tall as I am. This morning before school she cried for half an hour about her hair. I thought I was capable of raising her differently. Raising her in such a way that things like hair wouldn't matter.

For her birthday I stripped the wallpaper from her room. This is not beautiful either. Scrape away the layers of wallpaper and sand down the paint, and what is left but old, cracked walls, uneven. Ballet dancers suspended on a backdrop of lilac and green do not make this beautiful. They distract and make us notice less what is underneath. Eight hours of water, steam, and red hands removing first the vinyl cover, then the paper backing. She chose her own colours for her room. Burnt orange and gold. And this time I painted not papered her imperfect walls. Her room glows with her own sense of hope. Many times in the past week, I've gone into her room to shut off a light which wasn't on.

I will not say, " Where has the time gone?" I know

where. Time moves on the other side of sleep, and I have just woken. I crave quiet more than I used to. I'm surprised at how much I enjoy small tasks around the house. When I stand in front of the mirror, I recognize myself, though admit it's not the reflection I would have intended, but it's mine.

I couldn't have dreamt this.

OUTSIDE, the cat coils her body. Her purring has stopped. Snow is in the forecast. Night is calling.

I am tired of this grief, so I rake it up, make piles and put it into bags. I want to hear a story I've never heard before. A story that starts in the middle and has two possibilities, to move toward a beginning or an end.

SOMETIMES I WANT TO RETURN to the time when you first went missing. Your tracks fresh in my mind. I want the warmth of candles, the mercy of a birch fire. People say get over it, move on, get help. Or maybe it's my voice saying it. But I don't want to leave that long cold month where everything stopped except my breath. I don't want life to get back to normal, to abandon the longing that burns on its own wick. This is holy ground.

When I shut my eyes I stand above your body and draw a circle. Outside the circle, cars pass and friends walk by solemnly in procession. They hold bundles in their arms, their books, their most treasured possessions. They wear heavy coats and scarves to protect themselves from the harsh wind. They do not speak, not because they can't, but because there is nothing left to say about this. They hold out their hands, beckoning me. I shake my head, tell them I will join them later.

I look up at the night sky. In it there is a blessing of northern lights, a sweet greening of night next to the full round mouth of the moon. Constellations blink in their own conversations, and to them I whisper your name.

Acknowledgements

THANK YOU to the following people, places, and organizations for their generous support. Robert Priest and the Writers' Union of Canada Mentorship Program; the faculty and participants of the 1999 Banff Centre for the Arts Writing Studio; Beth Munroe for her early reading of the manuscript.

Always, to Eunice Scarfe for sharing her gifts and giving the most remarkable "voice lessons." Edna Alford, for her keen eye and wise, patient heart. Kerry Mulholland, Cathy Hodgson, Rebecca Schellenberg, and Beckie Garber Conrad and Wednesday afternoons; Susan Sharpe; Rae Watterworth; Jacqueline Bell. My sisters Terryl and Maxine; and Ted, Kirsten, Sarah, and Jesse, all of whom have shown me the many faces of courage. My mother and father who have walked this earth with great grace and dignity. Finally to Terry, Maeve, and Emily whose consistent light brightens the darkest days.

The book of poetry referred to on page 55 is Patrick Lane's *Winter*, Coteau Books, 1991. The truth "Any story twice told is fiction," paraphrased on page 57 is from Grace Paley.

Thank you to Tappan Wilder for permission of the Thornton Wilder quote.